A Church Girl's Guide to OVERCOMING Impulsive Spending

by

RHEA PARKS

Watersprings
PUBLISHING

Published by Watersprings Publishing a division of
Watersprings Media House, LLC.
P.O. Box 1284, Olive Branch, MS 38654
www.waterspringsmedia.com, Contact publisher for bulk orders and permission requests.

Copyrights © 2019 by Rhea Parks. All rights reserved.

All rights reserved. No part of this publication may be reproduced, distributed, or transmitted in any form or by any means, including photocopying, recording, or other electronic or mechanical methods, without the prior written permission of the publisher, except in the case of brief quotations embodied in critical reviews and certain other noncommercial uses permitted by copyright law.

Scripture quotations from THE MESSAGE. Copyright © by Eugene H. Peterson 1993, 1994, 1995, 1996, 2000, 2001, 2002. Used by permission of NavPress Publishing Group.

Scripture quotations credited to NIV are from the Holy Bible, New International Version. Copyright © 1973, 1978, 1984, 2011 by Biblica, Inc. Used by permission. All rights reserved worldwide.

Scripture quotations marked (NLT) are taken from the Holy Bible, New Living Translation, copyright © 1996. Used by permission of Tyndale House Publishers, Inc., Wheaton, IL 60189 USA. All rights reserved.

Scripture quotations marked AMP are taken from the Amplified Bible, New Testament Copyright © 1965, 1987, by the Zondervan Corporation. Used by permission. All rights reserved.

Printed in the United States of America.

Library of Congress Control Number: 2019912196
ISBN-13: 978-1-948877-28-2

Table of Contents

	Introduction	1
1	Spending Impulsively	4
2	Pay Them Bills!	9
3	The Anxiety of Money	12
4	The Emotional Roller Coaster	19
5	Negative Patterns = Self-Sabotage	23
6	Everything Ain't Always About You	26
7	Faith It!	32
8	Marriage Money	36
9	Saving God's Way	40
10	Tithing	44
11	Is Your Money of Service?	49
	Appendix: Additional Tools	53
	365 Financial Affirmations	56
	About The Author	77

To my husband, Ricky for allowing God to use me to be so transparent about my/our experiences with money. To Tasha, my tithing accountability partner. You came at just the right time and I am thankful. To my sons, Amir, Zion, Micah, Gavin, and Ricky, thank you for still loving mommy despite my faults. For being short-tempered with you for things you had no knowledge, or control over. Again, my husband, Ricky thank you is an understatement! Thank you for being completely on board just because I asked, and you love me. Thank you for believing in me, and this vision, even when I didn't, and couldn't. Thank you for allowing me to be the me that God needs me to be.

Prayer

*I decree and declare that you pay cash for everything!
His word says you are the lender and not the borrower.
You are the head and not the tail.
You are above and not beneath.
In Jesus' name AMEN!*

"Rejoice in the Lord always: again I will say, Rejoice.
- Philippians 4:4 ASV

Introduction

God's timing is extremely different from our concept of time. When your financial hardship hasn't ceased, that doesn't mean God hasn't heard your outcry for help. It just means there's more to learn of this lesson in this season. I remember waking up in the morning after I made an impulsive purchase being riddled with guilt, still trying to justify the purchase. I often ended up with tons of excessive material things, many still tagged and unworn. There were many days that I felt so tormented, not only because I had useless things, but because I maintained and kept up this façade. Nice, pleasant, and patient in public, but behind closed doors rude, nasty, and impatient with my own family. I was in constant clap-back mode!

The reality was, money and finances had me so tightly wound and stressed that I was cursing my kids out on a regular basis. Irritated for a multitude of reasons, but truly only having myself to blame for all of the financial stress. That is until my Heavenly Father intervened. It had gotten to the point that I had begun to feel so uncomfortable, almost shameful, about unnecessary purchases, and I knew this was the pruning of God. Then one day the light bulb went off. I needed to allow God to lead me with my finances. He needed to tell me how and when to spend my money. He would need to become my Counselor regarding my finances. There was no way I could make it happen on my own willpower. I could only be successful through, and with God. Success would come from meditating on God's word and letting Him show me and guide me.

It was always being on edge, stressed, and anxious that led me to my resource (the Bible) for my answers (remember when life's battles feel as though they are getting the best of you put a word on it!). Philippians 4:4-7 (ASV) states, *"Rejoice in the Lord always: again I will say, Rejoice. Let your forbearance be known unto all men. The Lord is at hand. In nothing be anxious; but in everything by prayer and supplication with thanksgiving let your requests be made known unto God. And the peace of God, which passeth all understanding, shall guard your hearts and your thoughts in Christ Jesus."* Before this, things had gotten really bad for me.

Right around the time we became intentional about purchasing our first home the enemy veered its ugly head. He knew right where to plant himself and show up. During this season of my life I became very miserable, which made me extremely short-tempered. I had even picked up social drinking again. I knew the enemy was working overtime on me. He made me feel unworthy of God's love and help. It made me feel like running away from my problems. The enemy has a way of making you feel as though you can't handle what's going on around you, but that's just his trick. He wants you to give up, but more importantly, he wants you to give up on God. He knows that God is far greater than any circumstance you may be going through and that is why he tries to trick you by playing mind games with you. I knew I was in what I call a 'testimony season'! I was "going through it" for a greater reason (a testimony for this book).

I often look back and remember how I felt that my boys' "bad behavior" made me a "bad mother". This period of time was filled with a lot of self-blaming. I worked a part-time job just to escape it all. The enemy has a way of highlighting your most vulnerable areas and making you believe and feel inadequate in those areas. But God has a way of using what the enemy meant to destroy you as a lesson to elevate you. So there was no escaping what I was running from. You see, you can't run from lessons that God is trying to teach you.

I knew deep down inside that this season I was in was for a purpose. I knew part of it was designed to strengthen me, but also a time to write and convey my experiences because I knew I wasn't the only one experiencing this. I wasn't the only one that emotionally felt like I was on a roller coaster. God always provides purpose to your struggles, you just have to be bold enough to share them. During this season of my life I was working on putting all the pieces of my financial experiences together, even the failures that came with impulsive spending, and that was a big one. During this time while I focused on our money and saving, I'd have these spending "relapses". One lapse even cost me almost $10,000, but it also helped me refocus on what I wanted versus what I needed. It was then that the Holy Spirit spoke and said, "Rhea slow down your thinking. Instead of marinating on things, marinate on My word." The quiet time allowed me to put things in perspective as well as understand where certain thoughts and dreams came from.

I long had dreams of owning a mixed-use building; commercial and residential. I never knew where this thought or dream came from but I will hold onto it and keep dreaming until it becomes my reality. You see, God will place things in your spirit during planting seasons that are so big, grand, outlandish, and over the top, that they help push you through that season. They also work as reminders of just how BIG God is.

1

Spending Impulsively

What would you do if the Lord whispered into your ear, "you're going to give your way out of debt?" Do you have enough faith to believe? Will you be faithful and follow the instructions? You do know, a part of faith is walking as though things already are? You see, God would always gave me a way out of making an impulsive purchase. I just rarely took it. I'd know when a purchase was made without consulting God first, because I would wake up the next day literally feeling sick to my stomach and bad about my decision. Or my first thoughts would pertain to how tight money was and how I couldn't afford what I had just purchased.

The crazy thing was, I would often ignore these thoughts and feelings and rationalize how "I really needed" whatever it was I bought. Many times, I would suffer in silence trying to balance the accounts (quite frankly we had too many, but that's covered later on in the book). At times, days and then even months would go by without me touching the item.

When I look back, I recall being in church in 2003 when a guest bishop, Bishop Joby Brady prophesied over my life. He told me that I'd own my own business, either individually, or family owned... something pertaining to women. He also said that I'd be wealthy. While I've held onto that prophecy for over a decade, I believe that prophesy and my misconstrued thinking around money has aided in my irresponsible and impulsive spending. Whenever I'd make an impulsive purchase I'd rationalize it by saying, "well I know I'll get through this, because God's already promised me that I'll be wealthy". Over the past decade I had to learn that God couldn't bless me more abundantly without me first demonstrating that I could effectively manage "the little". Luke 16:10 KJV states, "He that is faithful in that which is least is faithful also in much." How can God begin to trust us with more mula, chicken, scrilla, cheese, dinero, coins, or even paper, if we're stumbling over pennies?! Even with the freedom of choice that God gives each of us, we are still required to be good stewards of what He's blessed us with if we ever want more. For me, that meant acknowledging my poor stewardship with each impulsive purchase.

Everything was a "need" to me. If there was something that I wanted, I bought it. I never considered what bills were due. I didn't care that we were living paycheck-to-paycheck. When I saw something I wanted I would simply buy it, without a care in the world in that moment. However, that feeling was always fast fleeting. In that mental space everything was earmarked a need, even when it was merely a want. The reality was I never learned how to identify a need vs a want. It was a matter of needing to learn how to deny my flesh and submit to God's Holy instructions about money.

- What are you doing to position yourself to walk in God's plan for your life?
- Are there areas of overindulgence hindering you from walking fully in your purpose?
- Is this (thing) bringing you closer to God or pushing you away from God?
- Is there anything causing you to feel guilty or shameful?

I challenge you to take inventory over your life. You see, you can't change what you can't, won't, or don't identify. What are you doing to position yourself to walk in God's plan for your life? Are there areas of overindulgence hindering you from walking fully in your purpose? I know my impulsive spending was for me. I knew there was no way God would, or could bless me with more financially if I continued with this pattern of spending. Because I was aware of this and knew I needed to change, I was also seeking answers from God's people through books. I learned a long time ago there is nothing too lofty for God to bring to fruition, because His word says that He wants to bring life and bring it more abundantly. *"Now to Him who is able to [carry out His purpose and] do superabundantly more than all that we dare ask or think [infinitely beyond our greatest prayers, hopes, or dreams], according to His power that is at work within us,"* Ephesians 3:20, AMP. So, I knew God was capable of doing more than all of my wildest dreams. And since I have dreamt of great things; being able to tip the same as, or more than the bill; paying for kids' college tuitions; purchasing people cars with cash; and buying people houses. I knew I wasn't destined to live just a mediocre life. I just hadn't learned that in order to get to that place financially, it required structure, discipline, and order to tap into that abundance that God promised in His word. If you're struggling with the "how-to" you must seek God's answers in the Bible.

Every time I "fell short" of my temporal financial goals. I had a go-to book that I would always read in order to get back on track, *Solving Your Money Problems* by Pastor David Crank. It helped me put my spending under godly submission. While I learned great things from that book, I learned something else far more important. You see, the many books I was reading couldn't teach me anything if I wasn't spending time with my Heavenly Father. I had to learn what His word said about money and how to spend it in order to master and control it. At this point money had me, and controlled me. I needed to learn God's instructions about money.

Learning His instructions better equips us when we need to go before Him in prayer about our money. At some point, if you haven't already prayed about money, you will, and you'll need to be able to pray God's word back to Him about your finances. I learned that praying His word back to Him obligates our Father to do what His word says for us, and our finances. However, the only way to accomplish this is through spending time with God reading His word, seeking a more intimate relationship with Him. Because that's what He ultimately wants; greater relationship with you so that He can guide you. It's only through that relationship that you will gain a better understanding of how to use and spend your money (which He's blessed you with), in order to advance His kingdom. You do know that your money isn't merely for your own personal use? You see, it takes actual money, green, chedda, choppy, chicken to get certain things done within the kingdom. Your money isn't supposed to just be used for your own personal and selfish gain!

During this time of all this reading, I remember being prompted to pray, asking for forgiveness of my sins and for a cleansed heart. At first, I wasn't sure why I was supposed to pray this, but then God revealed that it wasn't for me, but it was so He could use me to intercede on your behalf financially! That couldn't happen if I was still living a financially challenged and broken life. Isn't it awesome and powerful knowing that God is capable of using perfect strangers to pray for your finances for you! I had to clean up my act financially for your good!

Your Action Step

- Based on the list created in the middle of the chapter, ask God to provide you with an effective plan to eliminate the things that are impacting your walk with Him, but most importantly effecting your financial situation. Ask Him to send it to you in a way that you will not second guess it and will know that it's coming from Him.

2

Pay Them Bills!

We all have purpose, it was given to us prior to birth. God is aware of each of us as individuals. We've all been hand-picked to complete a divine purpose that *only you* can accomplish and bring to pass. God highlights this individuality about each of us in Jeremiah 1:5 (NLT), *"I knew you before I formed you in your mother's womb. Before you were born I set you apart and appointed you as my prophet to the nations."* However, with divine purpose, also comes a higher level of interruption from the enemy. He's aware of your purpose and "he comes to kill, steal, and destroy" (John 10:10 NIV). In addition to impulsive spending, I also had a problem with paying bills on-time *all the time*. I am not sure of when or even how it had gotten to this point. The one memory that sticks out most vividly in my mind was being in grad school in 2006 and feeling this uncontrollable urge to spend my entire paycheck without having paid my rent yet. It was as if there was an uncontrollable pull to continue to swipe and spend until my bank account read $0. It was then that the rush and thrill began with the hunt and pressure of having to come up with my rent money. While I have been semi-successful with quenching that urge during certain periods of time, I had never truly addressed the root of the issue to my spending, I only buried it. But in time, it would rear its ugly head throughout my life.

Fast-forward to receiving a call from my children's dentist about an old bill. I remember having to check myself, because I was in the midst of catching an attitude because the office called requesting payment for an old bill. I remember thinking to myself, "how dare they call me asking for money". When I answered the phone, right after the thought, I heard the Lord say, "you did like their services when they were cleaning your kid's teeth, right?" "They did service ya'll!". In that moment, I quickly got myself and my thoughts all the way together. I had the audacity to get upset about having to pay for services that were rendered.

I knew there was no way that God was going to bless me financially, because quite frankly, I was way too messy! Struggling to pay all of my bills on time because I couldn't curb my impulsive spending. Along the way, I learned that not only did I need to pray and ask God for financial discipline, but also very simply, I had to STOP SPENDING MONEY I DIDN'T HAVE. There are lessons all throughout the Bible regarding financial accountability and how we are supposed to spend money. The principle regarding paying others for their services in 1 Timothy 5:18… "Those who work deserve their pay!" Find yourself an accountability partner if need be. Ask for Godly conviction; remember chastisement from God comes from love. Like parents yelling in order to protect their child from crossing the street without looking, God is no different when it comes to us. He wants what's best for us financially. If we're doing wrong and spending incorrectly isn't it God's duty to correct us?

This wasn't the only time that God needed to check me about my attitude toward paying my bills. I remember finding myself becoming upset when I forgot to pay my $25 a month student loan payment and the loan servicer would contact me seeking payment. I simply believed because it was such a small amount and I would forget to pay, the loan servicer didn't need to call me. Well I was wrong, and the Lord convicted me about that as well.

During this journey I learned that God's word can speak to every financial situation I found myself in. The Bible touches on doing things in decency and order in 1 Corinthians (NLT) 14:40, *"But be sure that everything is done properly and in order."* Paying your bills on time, all the time, is no exception to the rule.

Your Action Steps

- Read the prayer below out loud for 7 days. At the end of each day journal your first thoughts about money.

- Compare and contrast your thoughts as the days progress and highlight the major differences.

Pray

"Father God, I come before You repenting for all things I have not done in decency and order, and anything that's gone against Your word. Thank You for Your continued grace and mercy, for Your love despite my shortcomings as it pertains to money. I thank You that You have not given up on me even though I may have given up on myself at times. I thank You in advance for Your blessings that will seek me out. I thank You that my spending falls in line with Your word and with Your commands. I thank You for my future financial blessings, In Jesus' name amen!

3

The Anxiety of Money

I could live in this chapter for the entire book. This is where I spent the majority of time with money even when it came to me writing this book. Feeling anxious. I am not quite sure how, or when, or even why money created anxiety within me, but I wanted and needed it to stop. I noticed it brought so much joy to me when I was able to help others financially and even spend money on my children and husband, but at the same time it was causing me anxiety, angst, frustration, concern, anger, sadness, stress, depression, emptiness, and disconnection. Once I was able to identify all of the feelings that money was causing me to experience and feel; I finally felt there was some sort of light at the end of my financial tunnel.

Again, this goes back to "you can't change anything you do not, or will not identify". I had been successful in naming what it was, but how do you truly yield all of your anxiety and fear about money to God? I hadn't yet mastered that concept. However, I was able to yield things like; car troubles, concerns about our kids, areas I wanted my husband and I to grow in, finishing my second master's program, my next career path and even the success of my mobile app (Not Your Average Church Lady). I was even good at praying for other people and their situations. However, I continued to secretly struggle with my own feelings around and about money and how God fits into it all... There were some nights that I'd wake up in the middle of the night thinking about purchases I had made, or how we were going to save a certain amount of money (specifically 10K). I'd even wake up thinking about our budget. It had gotten to a point that even when I was directed by the Holy Spirit to give, or pour into someone else, I'd wake up the next day with anxiety about the decision. (Note: I knew it was the Holy Spirit telling me to give, because the amounts were always small and they never "broke the bank"; it was never our last dollar or even close to our last.) I knew those anxious thoughts were from the enemy, because God does not cause anxiety within His children.

My anxiety had gotten to a point where the money and our budget started to become my first thoughts in the morning. They had a way of secretly creeping into my mind and becoming rooted thoughts that would manifest themselves in my spirit. I remember developing three canker sores (caused by stress) within a week's span, because I was stressing and over-thinking about our finances. I was at a point that I was desperate for help. I needed it to stop. It was beginning to mess with my mood and the person that I was called to be. I want you to envision a tree; planted and rooted. Now think about it, with a tree you only get to see what is exposed above ground; the branches and leaves. However, that very same tree has roots deep beneath the ground. The things money afforded me, and my appeared presence was the tree and the leaves. Above ground, I looked like I was thriving financially; however, underneath my roots were being weakened by my anxiety around money, which stemmed from my thoughts and perceptions about money.

The interesting thing about God, faith, prayer and being a believer is once you understand and experience the power of prayer you can always rely on it during crunch time, or for me, during those anxiety-provoking financial moments.

A Church Girl's Guide to Overcome Impulsive Spending

Use the tree diagram below to label your deep rooted issues attached to spending.

Throughout these financial anxiety highs, I found several scriptures that provided me with some reassurance in Christ that I wasn't alone. Luke18:27 (KJV), *"And he said, the things which are impossible with men are possible with God".* Hebrews 11:1 (KJV), *"Now faith is the substance of things hoped for, the evidence of things not seen".* Are you bold enough to believe God about your finances? How about when what you're experiencing demonstrates differently? I remember wanting to buy a house so bad but hitting hurdle after hurdle. Then one day the Lord told me to write down exactly what I wanted in a home. He told me to be extremely detailed. There was some extreme hesitation and I knew why. I have a family of 5 growing boys; all of whom love to play football outside...ALL DAY, EVERYDAY! I was afraid of writing down the details in fear of God not being able to provide it, but He reminded me of Ephesians 3:20 yet again!

Philippians 4:6 (KJV) states, *"Don't worry about anything; instead, pray about everything. Tell God what you need and thank him for all he has done."* The New Living Translation reads, *"Do not worry. Learn to pray about everything. Give thanks to God as you ask Him for what you need."* I often found myself mentally walking on eggshells every time I thought about money. When I first read the passage my first thoughts were, "Rhea you'll be in prayer all day every day!", but slowly I began swapping in prayer and speaking this word over my life little by little, worry by worry.

Remain encouraged and know that God cares about you. He doesn't want to see you worrying about money. The Bible has knowledgeable gems all throughout it, 2 Corinthians 12:9 (MEV) *"My grace is sufficient for you, for My strength is made perfect in weakness. Therefore, most gladly I will boast in my weakness, that the power of Christ may rest upon me".* Psalms 34:17-18 (MEV),*"The righteous cry out, and the Lord hears and delivers them out of all their troubles. The Lord is near to the broken-hearted and saves the contrite of spirit".*

Learning to counter these thoughts with these scriptures took time because I wasn't wired to immediately think "pray". I taught myself, but more importantly I asked God to show me how to rely solely on His word during those moments. I'm not saying that the increased anxiety immediately went away; however, now I knew how to combat it. And combat it in a way that actually worked! Truly giving something completely over to God means you've left it resting at His feet and you've walked away. The difficulty in this for me is that I'm the type of person that needs to be able to wrap my head around how I'm going to get out of something. So, leaving something at God's feet for me meant leaving "a problem" unanswered, and that was a HARD PILL TO SWALLOW! But that is what faith is! My prayer is that through the course of reading this book, you'll learn and see that there is a scripture for everything under the sun about your finances. I pray that your faith begins to expand as you read. As your faith expands your worry will dissipate!

My experience has taught me that worrying over money will only increase my anxiety. Matthew 6:27 (NLT) highlights worrying, *"Can all your worries add a single moment to your life?"* Knowing they can't, why worry? During this season of my life I learned this was the enemy's way to keep me focused on other things. Being worried about our money made me lose focus on the ultimate prize! And that was the grace and favor that God was currently giving my family and His many blessings. It reminds me of the time when our Chrysler Town & Country had over 150K miles, our dashboard lit up like a Christmas tree, our transmission was in the process of going, and my mechanic had estimated that repair to be over $2,500. I prayed so hard over that car one rainy night. We still owed a little over $4,500 and when we attempted to trade it in we were offered only $1,500.

That rainy night I prayed that God would make it right, quick, fast, and in a hurry. I prayed that He would get us out of being financially top heavy for the car. I prayed for immediate debt cancellation. Now fast-forward to less than 7 days after that prayer. Our car was vandalized! Someone had taken it upon themselves to spray paint the entire car. Top to bottom and front to back. But when it was all said and done the car insurance company valued the repaint job at $8,000 but valued the car at $7,830. And just like that, we no longer had a car payment! We even had enough money to purchase something else cash out. No loan! God was able to use that catastrophe and turn it into a blessing. The lesson I learned was that God doesn't operate how I operate. When I prayed that prayer, I thought that somehow God was going to just allow the bank to forgive what we currently owed. But instead He allowed someone to destroy our van in order to bless us! So, remember that sometimes what looks like destruction is just God's way of setting you up for your very next blessing. Even when the situation doesn't look like it's going to work out in your favor just allow God to work in the background, because He's working it out for your best!

Your Action Steps

- Create a list of things that bring you joy and that you find pleasure in doing.

- Write another list of things you notice that create anxiety, negative feelings, or creates negative consequences in your life. Examples of potentially negative feelings: anger, frustration, stress, sadness, anxiety. After this list is created, work towards creating a realistic plan to eliminate these things.

4

The Emotional Roller Coaster

You see, our finances and money had me on an emotional roller coaster. It felt like I lived on this spectrum of extremes; going from 1 to 100 at the drop of a hat. I'm sure there were days that my boys asked themselves "what's wrong with Mommy?" I can even recall a number of times each of them asked me, "Mommy, you irritated?" Some days they were right on the money, while other days they were wrong. The days they were wrong truly made me do a self-evaluation about my attitude around the house... There were a number of non-financial things that I attributed my attitude and lack of peace to. Like, being a family of 6 living in a small 2-bedroom apartment with an eat-in-kitchen. There were days that not being able to eat at a dinner table set me off. There were other days that my boys having to do homework on the living room floor set me off. Other days it was because my kids were playing football in the living room and I was trying to watch TV, (there was no space for me to relax and them to play except the living room). Then there were days I was set off because I was ironing clothes on top of a dresser in the kitchen.

But ultimately it was all about money. Our living situation made me feel inadequate and less than as a mother. I often questioned my ability to be a "good mother". There were many days that I felt like a failure as a mother because I wasn't providing a more comfortable living environment for my children; a home for them to run around and play in. Often times, this made me feel uncomfortable, because I was forced to confront my own shortcomings when it came to managing money. God had a unique way of forcing me to face my mishandling of money and become accountable about my spending habits.

I remember being $1,500 away from saving $10,000; experiencing a move of God; and still continuing with my destructive impulsive spending. It was very awkward. God was instructing me to give and sow seeds, but at the same time I continued my dysfunctional spending patterns of impulsive shopping, throwing myself into panic mode. After which, I realized I spent over $3,000 within a matter of weeks. All of which directly affected my overall attitude and demeanor around the house. You see, the seeds I was sowing were producing what God said they would produce; an overabundance of blessings! I was receiving job offers, our weekly income was providing just as it should, with excess. But on the flip side, because I was continuing to spend irresponsibly while still trying to save according to God's devised plan, I was on a financial emotional roller coaster and it didn't feel good. I yearned for financial peace. You see, I was trying to serve two very different masters. God, and the enemy that fed my impulsive spending, which is impossible to do because both require your all. The Bible plainly states it in Matthew 6:24 (NLT), *"No one can serve two masters. For you will hate one and love the other; you will be devoted to one and despise the other. You cannot serve God and be enslaved to money."* And my impulsive spending kept me enslaved to money.

    I found peace after seeking God's word. I also experienced godly confirmation after having heard the voice of God regarding our savings. Remember, I told you we were only $1,500 away from saving $10K? Based on how we were saving we should have amassed the $10K in the summer, but due to continued impulsive and irresponsible spending on my part, that didn't happen. In a matter of 30 days God continued to speak to me. I kept hearing 90 days in my spirit. Initially I thought He was telling me that He would bring to pass home ownership in 90 days, which would have been the end of 2018. The 90 days didn't make sense until March 2019; 90 days from the time that an overabundance, overflow and saucer cup of financial blessings began to pour in. I had realized that we were never able to get qualified for a house prior to that because I was waiting for the overflow to begin. It was in that overflow that we would get prequalified for double the amount, because of the overflow that God was pouring into us. This move of God demonstrated that what I could not complete or accomplish in my own timeframe God was going to bring to pass in the next 90 days, but it would be done with His all-encompassing power. God needed to show me that He would be the one to get me to these goals; that my own will would not get it done. Being such an analytical person and needing to be able to mentally wrap my head around stuff in order to be able to "see it through", I knew God was stretching my faith, because at the time my current situation did not look like any of my goals would get completed in the span of 90 days.[1]

Throughout this financial journey I was able to learn something rather quickly, and that was, when I am in need seek my Heavenly Father and His word through the Bible. So, for my peace of mind I found Philippians 4:7 (AMP), *"And the peace of God [that peace which reassures the heart, that peace] which transcends all understanding, [that peace which] stands guard over your hearts and your minds in Christ Jesus [is yours].* Every time doubt crept in, because it often did, I prayed and looked to God to help me past my emotions. Because truth be told, I just couldn't do it on my own. I have experienced some really high highs and some extremely low lows during my financial journey. Throughout it all I have had to learn that I CANNOT DO IT ON MY OWN. That even when I think I have mastered how to spend money I still require God's daily guidance.

Having the tendency to get ahead of myself believing that because I haven't made an impulsive purchase in a few weeks or even months that I have it mastered, or that "I'm good" and "I got this saving and spending thing down", but quickly realizing that I don't is when my emotions can get the best of me. It's during those cocky, self-assuring moments that God demonstrates to me that it is not by my strength alone that I have it conquered, but rather through and with Him (Psalms 46:1 *"God is our refuge and strength, always ready to help in times of trouble").* When I think I have it (impulsive spending) defeated. God is always ever-present when we (His children) are in trouble. We just have to know His voice in order to follow His instructions.

Having a master's in Marriage and Family Therapy I fully understand the importance of not allowing emotions to dictate my actions. I understand the importance of not making an emotional decision. I understand how being led by emotions has fueled my impulsive shopping. I understand how not being able to deny my flesh, or deny my wants has led me into financial disarray. And because I am fully aware of all of these things and still make unwise financial decisions, just reassures me of just how much I need God to guide me daily in this journey.

---

1 The # 9 also signifies the perfect movement of God. It's also the number of patience.

Your Action Step

- Give yourself room for forgiveness. Know that you will make mistakes; some bigger than others and it's ok. By giving yourself permission to forgive yourself you will begin to create a space of peace. Forgiveness is the key to getting off the emotional roller coaster. It's your thought process of having to be perfect that keeps you on the emotional roller coaster.

5

Negative Patterns = Self-Sabotage

I often unknowingly self-sabotaged the mess out of our savings plan. Every time we neared a financial savings goal, I'd spend a *nice* chunk of money! There was always this eerie feeling of release when I'd fall short of the goal. I didn't recognize it until I started writing this book. Piece by piece, day by day, God began to work and deal with me. Nowhere along the line did I ever think trying to buy my first house would end up being documented and shared with the world! But my God did; He's just awesome like that. He's allowing my pain to connect, push, and elevate others. I depended and relied so heavily on God for this project. I only wrote when He told me what to write and when He gave me the words. This book is the evidence of God's guidance and His great faithfulness. It demonstrates His ability to use all of me. All of my faults, all of my shortcomings to get the victory from my story. It was only for the grace of God that I didn't lose it when I *lost* it financially, because the reality was, I was raggedy! At the end of the day I was forced to ask myself, did I want God's promise more than another pair of shoes?

Answering that question, I came to the realization that I wanted God's absolute best. Not His absolute best as it pertained to materialistic things but His absolute best for my life. Somewhere along the way I began to equate best as it pertained to my outward appearance. And being materialistic meant making sure that I had the absolute best shoes, the absolute best clothing, the absolute best hairstyle, the absolute best nails. It meant my boys had the absolute best school uniforms, the absolute best fall coats, the absolute best winter apparel. All these things related to our outward appearance. But what my Heavenly Father wanted for me was so much greater than all those carnal things. I learned that by seeking God's best it ensured all my financial needs would be well taken care of, as well as, the materialistic things too. The reality was that God knew who He created; a daughter that liked and enjoyed the finer things in life. I knew He would provide all of those things to me as long as I learned to continually put my Heavenly Father first and allow Him to order my spending.

While I learned *all these* great things about myself and my ability to self-sabotage, it wasn't the easiest lesson to learn. As humans we are all creatures of nature and we do what we know and what feels most comfortable..... sometimes unknowingly. The same rule of thumb applies with money. We spend and save according to our experience. My experience was spending until I had nothing left. If I am honest with myself this was a habit that had formed many years ago. When I look back I can recall when I got my first credit card as a senior in high school at only 17 years old. I was walking around our local college campus (Syracuse University) and completed a credit card application by lying about my age, but it worked. I was approved for a credit card and went to immediately maxing out the credit card. I had managed to pay it off before graduating from high school, but the damage and the pattern had already formed. This is how I managed and spent my money for the next 2 decades. My pattern was spend, spend, spend, and then scramble to devise quick ways to pay off what I had just spent. During those early years I just didn't make enough to pay anything off quickly, or even pay more than the minimum payment. Credit cards for me were the trap of the enemy and they kept me in a cycle of debt.

Your Action Steps

- Explore your early experiences with money. What patterns do you notice?
- How did the adults in your life use money?
- What was the model for you regarding money?
- Did you learn to be frugal?
- Did you learn to spend until nothing was left?
- Did you learn how to save?
- What generational patterns exist within your family— what did generation after generation do with money?
- How was it managed or mismanaged?

6

Everything Ain't Always About You

Somewhere along this personal journey I realized that the importance of this book wasn't about me at all, but rather about those that were connected to this book. I'm not sure who you are individually, but know that God has allowed me to experience some financial highs and lows to share through this book that are directly connected to you. It is only because of our Heavenly Father that we get to experience financial freedom. Remember, it's only because of His son, Jesus Christ that we are successful. My one and only request is that once you achieve this great feat that you share with others that it is only because of your Lord and Savior you are where you are!

I learned that a huge part of the journey is conceding to God along the way. That means, getting out of the driver's seat and allowing God to drive. It took me a while, but eventually I learned to lean on God.

Proverbs 3:5-6 (NLT) states, *"Trust in the Lord with all your heart; do not depend on your own understanding. Seek his will in all you do, and he will show you which path to take"*. For me that meant every time I had the urge to make an impulsive purchase. Every time I wanted to start a "new" business. Every time I wanted to change jobs. Every time I wanted to give and bless someone else. It meant talking to God first. Conceding meant giving all aspects of my finances over to God. It meant being ok with the unknown and not being in control. It meant being smart about purchases, which meant asking and conferencing with God first before something was paid for. It meant consulting with God before making any decision that would impact my finances.

I will be completely transparent and honest; the majority of my journey didn't feel good. Most of it was uncomfortable and foreign to me. I bucked a lot of the times, and even made purchases against God's will simply because I wanted something.

The longer I traveled this road, the more I came to learn through scripture that there was an uneven balance that I held between God and money. The way I was currently moving indicated that money was my master, especially when I made purchases despite God's advice. You see, it's unhealthy to attempt to serve two masters; in doing so you will quickly learn it's impossible.

Matthew 6:19-25 (NLT), *"Don't store up treasures here on earth, where moths eat them and rust destroys them, and where thieves break in and steal. Store your treasures in heaven, where moths and rust cannot destroy, and thieves do not break in and steal. Wherever your treasure is, there the desires of your heart will also be."* *"Your eye is like a lamp that provides light for your body. When your eye is healthy, your whole body is filled with light. But when your eye is unhealthy, your whole body is filled with darkness. And if the light you think you have is actually darkness, how deep that darkness is!* *"No one can serve two masters. For you will hate one and love the other; you will be devoted to one and despise the other. You cannot serve God and be enslaved to money."*

Trying to serve two masters only caused me stress, strain, and even more worry! It was only through this journey that I have learned different habits through the help of scripture.

I often found myself overthinking a lot of aspects to managing my money better, because remember, I *always* needed to be in control. But being in control only made me worry and fret. I didn't know it yet, but clearly, I didn't need to be the one in the driver's seat. The Bible provides us with provision and instruction regarding worry.

Matthew 6:26-34 (NLT), *"That is why I tell you not to worry about everyday life—whether you have enough food and drink, or enough clothes to wear. Isn't life more than food, and your body more than clothing? Look at the birds. They don't plant or harvest or store food in barns, for your heavenly Father feeds them. And aren't you far more valuable to him than they are? Can all your worries add a single moment to your life?* *"And why worry about your clothing? Look at the lilies of the field and how they grow. They don't work or make their clothing, yet Solomon in all his glory was not dressed as beautifully as they are. And if God cares so wonderfully for* wildflowers that are here today and thrown into the fire tomorrow, he will certainly care for you. Why do you have so little faith? "So don't worry about these things, saying, 'What will we eat? What will we drink? What will we wear?' These things dominate the thoughts of unbelievers, but your heavenly Father already knows all your needs. Seek the Kingdom of God[e] above all else, and live righteously, and he will give you everything you need. "So don't worry about tomorrow, for tomorrow will bring its own worries. Today's trouble is enough for today."

You have to learn to cast your cares and worries on the One who was intended to carry them, God. We often walk through life carrying past circumstances and experiences with us daily, when in fact, we were never supposed to pick them up. While they may have happened to us, we weren't supposed to carry the burden of the experience. I know for me, I carried around those memories of all those impulsive purchases as my own punishment for disobeying God, and even making the purchase. When I dug a little deeper, I realized I shopped every time I experienced failure; every time something didn't happen in my time. There was something about buying nice things that made me feel better. I quickly learned this was just a temporary fix to a deeper issue, which for me, was about a lack of self-esteem. For the majority of this journey I was trying to co-pilot with God and the reality was that He didn't need my help when it came to my finances, but rather I needed all of the help He was offering.

The lesson about semi-obedience is that it's still disobedience. I knew I didn't want to find myself being like the Israelites in pursuit of a promise from God that was supposed to take 40 days, but turned into 40 years in the wilderness, because of disobedience and unbelief?! My unbelief stemmed from my own lack of self-esteem and my own lack of ability. I often became frustrated when I was unable to complete or accomplish a task. I had to learn what the Bible speaks about seeking refuge in the Lord, because He is our source. He is our protector. He is our strength. He is our way maker. He is our miracle worker. He is our promise keeper. He is our redeemer. *Psalms 9:10 (NLT) states*, "The Lord is a shelter for the oppressed, *a refuge in times of trouble*". And also, in Isaiah 26:4 (NLT) it says, *"Trust in the Lord forever. For the Lord God is a Rock that lasts forever."* You see, while I would always let myself down, because I am not perfect and cannot do all things; however, my Christ is perfect (without sin) and able to do all things.

He is incapable of letting me down.

Psalms 34:17-18 (NLV), *"Those who are right with the Lord cry, and He hears them. And He takes them from all their troubles. *[18]* The Lord is near to those who have a broken heart. And He saves those who are broken in spirit."* 2 Corinthians 12:9 (NLV), *"He answered me, "I am all you need. I give you My loving-favor. My power works best in weak people."* I am happy to be weak and have troubles, so I can have Christ's power in me.

I'll be honest, some of my compliance wasn't because I truly wanted to comply, but rather fear of the consequences from God if I didn't comply kept me in line some of the times. When things didn't happen in my timing rather than become frustrated, I needed to learn it wasn't failure simply because it didn't happen based on my schedule. The real treasure is knowing that everything happens in God's timing and it's His timing that is always best for us. During this journey I would learn in many of those impulsive shopping moments that I was putting my own selfish desires ahead of those of my Heavenly Father and it's His promises for our life that eventually come to pass. Numbers 23:19 (NLT) states, *"God is not a man, so he does not lie. He is not human, so he does not change his mind. Has he ever spoken and failed to act? Has he ever promised and not carried it through?"* It took a while for me to make the connections, but those impulsive purchases made against God's will oftentimes lead me on a downward spiral. Disobedience earned me; discomfort, distress, and worry. I challenge you to ask yourself, what is your disobedience causing you?

Often times, we hear the word submission and immediately think, "I am too old to be submitting to anyone besides myself", or "I'm too grown to be listening to someone else." I knew I needed to learn to submit to God. Although it was my money, I needed to learn how to submit what God was blessing me with. There was a part of me that felt I was too old to be submitting to anyone other than myself; however, there is a huge difference in Godly submission. There's nothing wrong with submission when you understand the person you're submitting to will never steer you wrong. When that person only wants the very best for you. When you know that part of your submission is also for your protection and your greater good, the process of submission becomes a lot easier. The Bible talks about submitting your actions to God in Proverbs and Psalms. Proverbs

16:3 (NLT) states, *"Commit your actions to the Lord, and your plans will succeed."* And Psalms 37:5 (NLT) says, *"Commit everything you do to the Lord. Trust him, and he will help you."* How awesome is it to know that even when you relinquish your control and submit all of your finances to God that all your needs will still be met. God will never request of you to relinquish your control over your money to leave you high and dry and destitute. If you begin to wholeheartedly trust God with your finances, He will leave you better than He found you!

Your Action Steps

- Explore how sharing your testimony would be helpful or impactful to someone else.

- How is sharing your testimony helpful to you and your ability to overcome?

7

Faith It!

There were plenty of times during this journey that I had to simply, Faith It! There were times that things didn't add up, but I had to trust God. Trust His plan. I have the personality type that needs to *always* be in control. Always know how everything is going to work out, or even not work out because that required a Plan B, but that's not how faith works. The Bible states in, Hebrews 11:1 (KJV), *"Now faith is the substance of things hoped for, the evidence of things not seen"*. If we had it all figured out there wouldn't be any need for faith.

A prime example of "faithing it" was when I wrote the credit bureaus in an attempt to have my private student loans removed from my credit report after being reported as defaulted for 7 years. You see, I had no idea that God was going to instruct the lending bank to forgive and no longer attempt to collect on over $90K in student loans, but He did. I just simply followed the instructions of sending letters to all 3 bureaus; one I had to send to multiple times until they finally stated that it hadn't been a full 7 years yet and I had to wait a few more months. It was shortly after that, that I received the letters advising they were no longer going to attempt to collect. That's exactly what "faithing it" looks like. Following the instructions even though everything around you appears differently. There were plenty of times that I questioned, "what happens if I don't have enough faith? Or even, "how much is enough faith?" But when in doubt, I always looked to my Bible for my answers. Matthew 17:20 (NIV), *"…. Truly I tell you, if you have faith as small as a mustard seed, you can say to this mountain, 'Move from here to there,' and it will move. Nothing will be impossible for you."* Imagine if your faith was as tiny as 1 minuscule seed? But yet, even in that tiny amount it's still powerful enough to move God to act on your behalf and work things out! His requirements of us are at the very least, minimal. Yet grandiose gestures from God are the final results! Have the words not convinced you yet?! Let's proceed.

Luke 12:7 says, *"But [even] the very hairs of your head are all numbered. Do not be struck with fear or seized with alarm; you are of greater worth than many [flocks] of sparrows."* I thought to myself while I wrote this book, surely if God cares enough to know the number of hairs on my head He won't disappoint or let me down in the midst of me "faithing it". Take the time and think about it, actually think about it. When you see the image above, imagine having to count the individual hair strands. God cares that much about you as an individual. He not only knows how many hairs are on your head, but He is also very aware of when you take "leaps of faith" and are believing in Him when it comes to your finances.

There were plenty of days that I awoke and looked at my immediate surroundings, which for the most part looked nothing like what God had promised me, or even what I was believing God for. But there's that "faithing it" thing again; continuing to believe in what God promised you despite what it looks like around you. I am not going to lie and tell you that that there weren't moments of frustration and sheer desperation to get out of my current situation, but I continued to hold onto those things that I prayed for and continued to believe God. What I did learn along my journey is that it was imperative to have other faith believers in my inner circle during times when my faith tank was low. Their ability to remain faithful and believe God, worked as my reserve tank. When my faith tank was running low I was able to tap into their faith to remain afloat.

"Faithing it" is similar to jumping out of an airplane and not having checked to verify that your parachute is operable, but knowing that it's going to support you during your descent. At some point, you're going to just have to jump! Jump for what God has promised you. Jump for what you're believing God to do. Jump in the direction of Godly intuition. Just jump. Jump knowing that despite what you're seeing and despite what you're experiencing that God's going to open the parachute, which will allow you to soar to His next level. But remember, you'll never be able to achieve or reach this new level without JUMPING first! For me, I needed to keep God ahead of me during this journey. I needed Him to canvas the area before I got there. During this journey with each mishap I often thought about the story of the Israelites and making a journey that should have only been 40 days, but due to disobedience and incorrect steps it took them 40 years.

"Faithing it" is walking with God even when you don't understand or know how He is going to bring a promise to pass. It's about blindly following God even when your current circumstances don't align with the promise. "Faithing it" is planting seeds and knowing that you will reap your harvest in "dew/due" season because that's simply how God operates. Galatians 6:9 (AMP) says, *"Let us not grow weary or become discouraged in doing good, for at the proper time we will reap, if we do not give in."* I encourage the eyes that are reading this right now, stay the path that our God has you on. TRUST THE PROCESS, it may not make any sense in this current moment, but I promise you there is always purpose to what you're going through. Lean on God and believe with your soul that IT WILL ALL WORK OUT. Now keep pushing you've got a race to finish.

Your Action Steps

- Read and meditate on Romans 8:28, "And we know that in all things God works for the good of those who love him, who have been called according to his purpose".

- The lesson is that God is able to use everything you experience; good or bad. Begin to think about some of your "bad" experiences and how God turned them around. Look for the lessons learned, or benefits gained from those experiences.

8

Marriage Money

I remember constantly thinking, and even saying out loud to my husband how moving out of the small box that we lived in and into a home with more space would make me happier. Then one day I said out loud what the Lord spoke to my spirit? "A house with more space isn't going to make you happier!". Saying it out loud made it real. As long as it stayed in my head I didn't have to acknowledge how truthful it was. Coming to this harsh reality for me was like ripping off a band-aid from a fresh wound.

We probably didn't get the finance thing right until about year 11 of our marriage. You see, I walked into the marriage an impulsive spender. And not that my husband was an impulsive spender; he just didn't know how to tell me no. I can recall taking a trip to Toronto to attend a pop-up shop for one of my favorite shoe designers, Jennifer Le to buy a pair of $450 boots. I knew we couldn't afford them but I wouldn't take no for an answer from my husband about purchasing them. Even though we had a joint bank account, we also both kept a separate checking and savings account that we individually had money going into. My problem was that I often looked at money as "his" and "mine". I just figured I had the money from my paycheck, in my account.

I needed to learn that although we were working and earning a living, the money wasn't truly ours, but rather God's. There was purpose to how our money was supposed to be spent. Our money wasn't merely for the purpose of buying more materialistic items, but rather a higher purpose attached to God. I needed to learn how to live and spend within our financial means; not lavishly above. I needed to learn that our money's most important use was to bring glory to God's kingdom. While God is capable of doing anything; the reality is that within this natural realm money is needed to accomplish many things within the kingdom.

Around this time I also came to the realization that there was never going to be the "perfect" time to get our finances in order. There would always be mishaps, wrong turns and even money screw ups as long as I was in the driver's seat. I truly needed to learn how to yield to God and ultimately turn down a good sale, and "the perfect shoe". Turn down my flesh and say no to my carnal desires for a great pair of shoes and hot outfit. It's not as if I was going to be able to take all that stuff to heaven with me. I couldn't even pass any of it down to my boys. You see, clothes ain't no inheritance.

I remember being awakened out of my sleep one time at 4:30 in the morning with the thought of needing to be more strategic with my money. I knew it was from God because that's how He always gave me ideas. It would be an immediate and sudden idea that would come to mind; it would either wake me up in the middle of the night, or be my first thought in the morning. Because I knew it was from God, I either had the choice of asking for His assistance and writing it down, or simply rolling back over and going to sleep. I'm a visual person, so I knew I needed to ask God to literally show me how to do it and not just drop the idea into my spirit.

God provides clear instructions on money and even inheritances throughout the Bible. *Proverbs 13:22 (AMP) states, "A good man leaves an inheritance to his children's children, And the wealth of the sinner is stored up for [the hands of] the righteous"*. But in order to do that I needed to become savvier, more strategic, and more God-lead when it came to spending money.

God has given each of us the freedom of choice. Your finances and even mine are no different. Just like I had the option of doing it my way, so do you. You can continue to do as I did, which resulted in continued failure, or you can begin doing what I finally did and that's asking God for His help to intervene. The same way He intervened and pulled me out of where I was drowning He will do the same for you; you just have to ask. It's God's wisdom that's needed to counter impulsive spending. Because there will be days, moments, months that are complete epic failures and it's Him that gives us provision and strategy to overcome the impulsivity within us.

For me there were many times throughout this journey that I

wanted to quit because I couldn't seem to get it right. Some days I felt as though I had this gigantic black cloud hanging over me. I never really noticed the black cloud because I was constantly in the "robbing Peter to pay Paul" mode. There was always this constant anxiety around not having enough money. There was never any peace for me around money until I started tithing faithfully. While there were always unexpected expenses coming up, I always justified them because I knew I wasn't doing right with my money (consistently tithing). But even once I "fully" got on board with the Word, (what I felt was applicable to me at the time) it still seemed like I couldn't catch a break. There was still very little peace with me and money. And that's because I was still in the driver's seat! I think I finally got out of the driver's seat after we purchased another van.

So, remember the spray painting of the van in the previous chapter? Well it doesn't stop there. The first 2 months of having the new van the gear shift broke, it overheated, and wouldn't pass inspection. Frustrated was an understatement! I had even traded in my beloved Dodge Charger and put up $2000. That season truly taught me that God would provide all my needs. There were times I wanted to pray but didn't for unimportant reasons. Then I remember a conversation I had with my brother and he reminded me that we have the power to manifest our own destiny. While I was very aware of this fact. I would just apply this mind frame to positive manifestations. After thinking about it I realized I was manifesting my own financial woes. I was always thinking about spending and being in constant lack. I needed to manifest saving, building wealth, and leaving an inheritance to my children's children.

Your Action Steps

- If you're married, or in a relationship write down you and your partner's financial strengths and weaknesses. Are there more similarities or differences?

- Begin to explore ways that will allow you as a couple to work more collaboratively with each other for the benefit of finances.

    - Examples: Are one of you better at managing the overall cash flow: input and output?

    - Paying all the bills? Monitoring the savings account?

9
Saving God's Way

Saving money is something that I've always struggled with, but it came second nature to my husband. We experienced what felt like roadblocks trying to save our first $3,000 and then our first $10,000. I remember amassing our first $10,000; there was something so exhilarating and so financially liberating about it. Being able to accumulate and save that amount of money in our account was such a huge feat for us; at least for me. Up until that point, I had only been able to save $1,000 and that was the summer going into my junior year in college. So, it had been over a decade-and-a-half that I had been able to save any amount of money. Everything up until this season in my life had been paycheck-to-paycheck.

What was so liberating is we didn't have any immediate use for it. Knowing it was in the bank made me move differently. It drastically changed my outlook and perception about money. I finally felt like I had managed to "master" money and not have money "master" me. Even though it didn't happen overnight, it eventually happened. I had to learn how to not rush the process. I needed to become more patient with the rate at which we were able to save money; despite always wanting everything to happen quickly. With saving money, I learned there was no quick way to save large amounts of money, but rather with patience and time it would accumulate. This process not only strengthened my patience, but taught me how to budget, save, and not spend impulsively. This was the interactional change that needed to happen for me and money. It was the change that changed my financial trajectory, but I was only able to do it with the help of God and by following His instructions.

Often times, I was looking for the quickest way out of financial hardships. To be perfectly honest, my brain had warped the message

I received from Bishop Joby Brady so many years ago that I would always just assume that God would "get me out" of all those financial hardships...even with credit card debt. Through saving I learned there was no "quick fix" which was how I often tried to pay our credit cards off (in large lump sums) and save money. I would always want the debt to go away quick, fast, and in a hurry. Through learning myself, my money habits, and my money addictions I learned that that was just my way of trying not to have to make any sacrifice to get rid of the debt. Looking back on it all, it's actually rather comical how my brain would rationalize and think, and over think extreme ways to pay those credit cards off.

I'll tell you, saving that first $10,000 didn't come without sacrifices and it didn't come without giving God His 10% off the top (tithing)! It also didn't happen with continued money mismanagement, and it certainly didn't come without the help of God and His word (the Bible). The Bible talks about impulsiveness and its consequences. Proverbs 14:29 (AMP) says, "...*But he who is quick-tempered (impulsive) exposes and* exalts his foolishness [for all to see] and Proverbs 21:5 (AMP), "*The plans of the diligent lead surely to abundance and* advantage, but everyone who acts in haste comes surely to poverty". It's plainly stated. Once you read it, you can either adhere to it and ask God to help you through the process, or you can choose to ignore His clear instructions and continue to spend impulsively, frivolously and continue to be financially strapped.

It was crazy how when I wasn't consistently tithing we would have these random expenses that always caused us to veer off our budget and savings pattern. However, once I started to tithe consistently (that meant EVERY pay date, even when we were out of town and not at church) I noticed we always had enough to pay everything due that week. Even when there were unexpected expenses, God always allowed us to have enough in addition to our tithe. For me that meant getting an accountability partner. Thank you, Tasha! The Bible also covers the tithe in Leviticus 28:30 (MSG) *"A tenth of the land's produce, whether grain from the ground or fruit from the trees, is God's. It is holy to God. If a man buys back any of the tenth he has given, he must add twenty percent to it."* For many people this may be a struggle, but I want to encourage you to trust God wholeheartedly, with all of your money. I have witnessed God provide us with more earning opportunities when we tithed faithfully. Literally the more we gave, the more God poured back into our bank accounts. He began blessing us on our jobs. My husband was being offered an abundance of overtime at his job to the point where he was having to turn some of it down. I experienced a job change that came with a higher salary. I also had a full caseload at the private practice I worked at while in pursuit of obtaining my clinical hours toward becoming a fully licensed marriage and family therapist. So, I am a witness to His ability to make your cup overflow.

I fully understand how hard it may be for you to completely trust in a God you cannot physically see, nor touch (that's what faith is), to help you manage and save your money. The reality is that you know you better than I know you. You know where your financial struggles lie better than I do; however, your Creator knows you even better. He created you. Jeremiah 1:5 (MSG) states, *"Before I shaped you in the womb, I knew all about you. Before you saw the light of day, I had holy plans for you."* So while you may think and believe that you can do it all on your own, you simply cannot! You must invite and walk in tandem with God along your journey. Begin to trust Him completely. Rely only on God and His financial plan for you. Not your own.

Your Action Steps

- For the next 7 days journal what the hardest part of letting go is for you.

- Begin to identify what barriers prevent you from allowing God to fully lead your financial journey.

- At the conclusion of each day of journaling stand in front of the mirror and repeat these words *"I am worthy of God's overabundance. It doesn't matter how much I may have messed up my money in the past. God does not care about that, that is my issue. Today I forgive myself for mismanaging my money. I forgive myself for spending recklessly and impulsively, because God already has. He wants to help me. He wants to see me living in His excess. I am no different than those that are wealthy. I am capable of obtaining wealth, because God's word instructs me to leave an inheritance for my children's children. To be the lender and not the borrower. Today I give God full reign over my money!*

10

Tithing

I remember trying to complete this chapter and getting stuck. Feeling as though I'd never be able to come up with the "right" words to say; in order, to "convince" those that read this to tithe; so, I'm not going to do that. I'm not going to brow beat you about the importance of tithing. I am going to simply demonstrate the importance of tithing through personal stories and testimonies and allow God to do the rest. The rest being, conviction if need be.

I've always known and understood the importance of tithing, but to put it nicely, I would just disregard it when it didn't 'fit' into my budget. So, year after year I'd accomplish minimal financial success on my own. I'd know that I needed to tithe consistently, but for some reason I just couldn't get out of my own way and rely entirely on my faith in God and His word as it pertained to the biblical principles about tithing. Despite going to church every Sunday and hearing other people's testimonies about how God continued to provide and provide more abundantly in their lives, because of their giving I still lacked faith in this area of my life.

I recall struggling with tithing at the top of 2018. At the advice of a prayer call I obtained an accountability partner (I can't thank Tasha enough, yet again). I began tithing faithfully via text and screen shooting the image to my accountability partner like clock-work every Thursday or Friday depending on the pay week. I even went as far as changing my banking info through the text-to-give app to my debit card instead of my bank routing number. I was so frivolous and impulsive with money I needed my transaction to pend immediately instead of not pending at all, and coming out a few days later. I had the tendency of forgetting about transactions and spending money that really wasn't available in my account.

For me, I needed to include tithing as a part of my weekly bills due. This way made it more manageable, but more importantly it made it a PRIORITY! You see, I had the tendency to pay God last. Meaning, I would pay all my bills before Sunday rolled around, which often times lead to miscellaneous spending before church. This had a trickle-down effect, because I often ended up not having enough money for tithing because of weekly mismanagement and impulsivity. Once I finally developed a system that worked for me, I began to experience the benefits of God's Word as it pertained to tithing.

> *Luke 6:38 (NIV)*
> *"Give, and it will be given to you. A good measure, pressed down, shaken together and running over, will be poured into your lap. For with the measure you use, it will be measured to you."*

Testimony 1: I remember being eight months into tithing faithfully. By faithful, I mean every penny of extra money that came into our household I tithed 10% like clock-work. I recall looking for another job in order to begin working toward obtaining my clinical hours to become a licensed marriage and family therapist. The job change really was not a big deal because there wasn't a huge change in pay; however, I had only received one job offer and it was a slight pay cut and minimal clinical hours despite having applied to over a dozen jobs. Then *suddenly*, I had one more interview for a therapist position at a private practice. Can you say HIRED ON THE SPOT! The beautiful thing was this job offer entailed working part-time hours (20) but earning the same amount as my then full-time job. In just one swift move God doubled my current salary! The beautiful thing was He blessed me abundantly. Not only did I receive a part-time job making the same amount as my full-time job, but the job offers continued to roll in. When it was all said and done I was offered 4 in total! You see, God provided an overflow and saucer cup blessing. Not only was I offered more than one position, but I had to turn down some of the offers!

Testimony 2: I remember attending our annual Women of Promise: On the Move Conference. I had sowed a few financial seeds on behalf of a woman I knew who had recently been let go from one of her jobs (primary income source), and was stressed out about making ends meet. Within two weeks of sowing those seeds I remember her calling me, because she was stressed out over which job she should take. Not only had she been offered a job at one of the local hospitals, which she had been trying to get into for a while now, but was also rehired at the place that let her go a week prior..... but with more pay! To top that off, there was a 3rd offer working another private case as a home health aide! Oh, to be overwhelmed and bombarded by God's overflow and abundance I am a firm believer that had I not shown myself faithful to what God was already blessing me with, He wouldn't have honored my seed on her behalf. You see, how could I ask Him to bless my seed if I wasn't being obedient with my tithe?!

Testimony 3: I remember early on when I first tried to tithe on a regular basis and I decided I also wanted to try and get my credit together. I went and got copies of three of my credit reports only to see that I had over $90k in private student loan debt showing negatively on my credit report. There all $90,000 of it was highlighted under: ACCOUNTS IN COLLECTIONS. I immediately felt a sinking feeling in my stomach, but I was determined. I immediately went to work and began writing the credit bureaus. I spoke earlier in the book about how that turned out.

Testimony 4: At this point I had been tithing just shy of a year. We were in a season of God's favor and abundance (what Pastor Godlock coined "a saucer cup blessing"). My husband was being offered overtime on his job for over 90+ straight days. I had a full caseload at the private practice I was working at. It had gotten to the point that I was needing to turn down new clients and he was having to walk away from overtime hours. The blessings came as our weekly income increased so did our tithe amount. I remember sharing with Tasha that I knew God was stretching us, because we were at the point that our tithe was exceeding my comfort zone. I didn't realize it until I had a conversation with my husband that I had become complacent at our current level of giving. With the increased income there were some weeks that our tithe was exceeding $400. You see, I began to notice the more we tithed the more God blessed us. That's the principle of sowing and reaping. If you give, (sow) according to scripture, then God allows you to reap what's due to you, your harvest! Luke 6:38 (NIV) says, *"Give, and it will be given to you. A good measure, pressed* down, shaken together and running over, will be poured into your lap. For with the measure you use, it will be measured to you." My giving was being measured and I was receiving back according to what I gave. God honors His word. You are not exempt to God's word. Trust and He will always deliver according to that word!

I often hear people asking, am I supposed to tithe on my gross or net income? My answer is, do you want a net blessing from God or a gross income blessing? For me that meant tithing based on our gross incomes. Tithing is about having enough faith in GOD to know that He will meet all of your needs when you follow His instructions.

My prayer for those that are reading this book that may be struggling with tithing according to the Bible is that you stretch your faith and believe in God's word. Pray these words:

Father God I come before You thanking You in advance for my obedience to Your word. Thanking You for Your grace and Your mercy. I thank You that I am a faithful tither and that You honor Your word within my life. I thank You that where I sow I will also reap. I will reap a bountiful harvest. I thank You that because I honor Your word I find favor in all areas of my finances, because Your word tells me that I am the lender and not the borrower. I am the head and not the tail. I am above and not beneath. As I give, it will be given back to me in good measure and for that I give thanks and honor
in Your Son's name. Amen.

Your Action Steps

- Do the math and calculate 10% of your gross income.

- Make that amount your next tithe amount. If when you add that amount and your other bills exceeds the actual amount you have coming in that week, do a thorough review of where your money is going.

- Begin to look for areas you can decrease your spending. An example would be: your monthly cell phone bill is $229, but your you're paying a $60 monthly charge for "leasing" the phones. The pay-off amount for the phones is $180 and you can own them. By "owning" the phone you would decrease your monthly cell bill to $169 from $229. This equals a more long term savings allowing you to be able to reallocate the $60 to another bill (credit card bill), without actually increasing the amount of money you have coming in.

11

Is Your Money of Service?

God is capable of blessing you beyond your wildest dreams financially Ephesians 3:20 (AMP) states, "Now to Him who is able to [carry out His purpose and] do superabundantly more than all that we dare ask or think [infinitely beyond our greatest prayers, hopes, or dreams], according to His power that is at work within us", but what use is it if it's not helping advance HIS kingdom? Well none really. It's similar to the closed fist analogy. If your fist is so tightly closed (hanging onto your money), so that you don't lose anything, then it's also so tightly closed that nothing is capable of getting in. Are you using your money to help others within the kingdom?

I've always been a giver when it came to money. Always willing to bless those around me through money. There has always been something about it that has brought me so much joy. I learned a long time ago that I had to use my money to help bless others if I wanted God to continue to pour into me financially. I have witnessed giving more and then ultimately receiving more from God! This takes me back to the parable in the Bible about the master that disbursed talents to his workers.

Matthew 25:14-30 (MSG) says, **14-18** *"It's also like a man going off on an extended trip. He called his servants together and delegated responsibilities. To one he gave five thousand dollars, to another two thousand, to a third one thousand, depending on their abilities. Then he left. Right off, the first servant went to work and doubled his master's investment. The second did the same. But the man with the single thousand dug a hole and carefully buried his master's money.* **19-21** *"After a long absence, the master of those three servants came back and settled up with them. The one given five thousand dollars showed him how he had doubled his investment. His master commended him: 'Good work! You did your job well. From* now on be my partner.' 22-23 "The servant with the two thousand showed how he also had doubled his master's investment. His master commended him: 'Good work! You did your job well. From now on be my partner.' 24-25 "The servant given one thousand said, 'Master, I know you have high standards and hate careless ways, that you demand the best and make no allowances for error. I was afraid I might disappoint you, so I found a good hiding place and secured your money. Here it is, safe and sound down to the last cent.' 26-27 "The master was furious. 'That's a terrible way to live! It's criminal to live cautiously like that! If you knew I was after the best, why did you do less than the least? The least you could have done would have been to invest the sum with the bankers, where at least I would have gotten a little interest. 28-30 "Take the thousand and give it to the one who risked the most. And get rid of this "play-it-safe" who won't go out on a limb. Throw him out into utter darkness.'

God has quietly entrusted *all of us* with gifts and talents to benefit us individually, but ultimately to advance His kingdom and bring glory to His name! So, how are you using what God has entrusted you with? Are you like the one, too afraid to use what God has already given you, that you either bury it or keep it so tightly closed no one can benefit from it? Your time, talents, and treasures…. all belong to God. We weren't individually blessed with our talents to only benefit and use for ourselves. Use your talents to help others along their journey.

Along the way I learned that one of my gifts is my compassion and empathy for others (sometimes it even scares me). But you see, it's those two things that God has blessed me with that allows me to interact and engage with people in a very special way that allows me to optimize my skill set as a therapist. I am fully aware that it's something that could have only been gifted from God and I use it accordingly; that is, one of my gifts. You see, the gifts that God bestows upon each of us, is also directly linked to our ability and power to obtain wealth using these gifts!

Through the compassion that God has placed inside of me coupled with my willingness to give to others financially, He continues to expand my boundaries; allowing me to reach others so that He gets the glory. Deuteronomy 8:18 (NLT) states, *"Remember the Lord your God. He is the one who gives you power to be successful, in order to fulfill the covenant, he confirmed to your ancestors with an oath"*. God wants to see each of His children successful and living a life of abundance, but it isn't going to magically happen. You're going to have to tap into God so that He may show you what your gifts are that you may begin to utilize them to obtain wealth. Always remember, it is not merely for your own good, but rather for the good of God's kingdom and helping build it! Watch how much more God will begin to bless you with when you give to others. I love that there isn't a designated amount that you're ordered to give. We are all able to bless others in small amounts, but are we willing to open ourselves up to the opportunity?

You can bless someone when you're ordering food through the drive-through. Simply pay for the order behind you. You can buy the person's groceries standing in front of you at the check-out line. You can take care of a co-worker's lunch bill. You can offer to pay someone's phone bill. Randomly sow a seed to someone's Cash App. There are a million and one different ways you can bless someone else. The beautiful thing is that God allows each of us to bless others based upon what we have individually He's happy with that. He doesn't compare our blessings to anyone else, but there is an expectation to bless based upon what you do have. I pray that you begin to expand your faith in the area of your finances. I pray that you begin to boldly give to others without the expectations of a gift in return. Give to those you know are not in the position to give back to you as your reward is stored up in heaven. Allow God to bless you for your ability to be a blessing to someone else.

Philippians 4:19 (NIV), "And my God will meet all your needs according to his glorious riches in Christ Jesus."

Remember God knows your financial situation inside-and-out. You are not fooling, hiding, or deceiving God of anything. So I end by encouraging you to allow God in the midst of the journey. Let Him help you pick up your individual pieces. It's in the middle of your struggle that God does His best work! 2 Corinthians 12: 9-10 (NIV), *"But He said to me, "My grace is sufficient for you, for My strength is made perfect in weakness."* Therefore most gladly I will boast in my weaknesses, that the power of Christ may rest upon me. So I take pleasure in weaknesses, in reproaches, in hardships, in persecutions, and in distresses for Christ's sake. For when I am weak, then I am strong".

Your Action Steps

- Begin to look for small ways to bless someone else financially. Let God direct you. Begin to wait in expectation of the Holy Spirit to tell you the who, what, when, and how to bless others.

- The Bible is a blueprint on how to live. If we study God's word and meditate on the words (consistently think about its instructions), we will be successful in all areas of our lives. It will cause us to be successful wherever we go!

Appendix

Additional Tools

3 keys to prosperous living according to the Bible:
Biblical background from Joshua 1:8 and Psalms 1:1-3

Tend – we must work. Nothing earned in life comes for free. We must work the talents that God has given us in order to be fruitful in life.

Keep – demonstrate good stewardship over what we've earned through our works. You have to know what to do with what you have. Being wasteful is not an option.

Give – Remember it's not always about you. You're supposed to use what you have to be a blessing to others. It's the concept of sowing and reaping. The more you give, the more God will bless you with.

Credit Letter used:

Upon reviewing my credit report (enter credit account #, which is at the top of your pulled report), I discovered an obsolete account (Original account creditor) ENTER ACCOUNT # FROM CREDIT REPORT. Please delete this account immediately as it is too old to be in my credit file. If for some reason the account is verified, please send me the name of the person who provided the information and the method in which it was investigated.

This according to FCRA §605 (c) 1 & FCRA §605 (A) 4
Key Bank (Account # XXXX-XXX-X1234). Delinquent date with Key Bank: November 2008. 180 days delinquent (May 2009).

Here I entered the original creditor, account #, and date it became delinquent with original creditor.
 I also provided the 180 days' delinquent month and year because my credit report had the wrong date.

Your Name

365 Financial Affirmations

1. I am changing my beliefs about money.
2. I always find a way to make money with God's help.
3. I am attracting money and growing my bank account.
4. I am a finely-tuned money making machine.
5. I am completely dedicated to acquiring more money to help do God's work.
6. I am totally focused on achieving financial success.
7. I am attracting large amounts of money into my life.
8. Money is everywhere around me.
9. I believe in myself and my ability to acquire massive wealth.
10. I have only positive beliefs about money.
11. I will change my beliefs about money.
12. I will be the kind of person who is always making money.
13. I am becoming wealthy.
14. I am beginning to feel that I truly deserve to be wealthy.
15. My attitude towards money is becoming more positive with each day.
16. Money is becoming easier and easier to acquire.
17. My mind is starting to feel highly attuned to money.

18. I will become fully dedicated to achieving financial success.

19. I will develop rock solid confidence in my ability to make money.

20. I am transforming into someone who allows God to direct and order my money.

21. I am just naturally good with money.

22. I deserve to be wealthy and have financial freedom.

23. I have an intense dedication to acquiring large amounts of money to advance God's kingdom.

24. My mind is naturally focused on making money to be a blessing to someone else.

25. I recognize that God and money work together for my benefit.

26. I find it easy to think positively about money.

27. I am effortlessly focused on money and God.

28. Money is all around me, all I have to do is reach out and grab it.

29. I think positively about money and this naturally attracts wealth into my life.

30. I am wealthy.

31. I always have money.

32. I attract financial abundance.

33. I always think positively about money.

34. I have many financial opportunities.
35. I am rich and prosperous.
36. My life is full of abundance.
37. I am focused on achieving wealth.
38. I am becoming wealthier.
39. My bank account is always growing.
40. Money will be flowing into my life.
41. I am finding it easier to attract money.
42. Financial opportunities are coming my way.
43. I will be financially successful.
44. I will attract wealth into my life.
45. Positive thinking is beginning to attract money into my life.
46. My positive attitude is beginning to attract large sums of money.
47. Attracting money is easy.
48. I effortlessly attract abundance.
49. I deserve to be wealthy.
50. My bank account never seems to stop growing.
51. I am highly focused on achieving financial success.
52. I fully believe in my ability to attract money.
53. I have a money mindset. Money just always seems to come my way.

54. I am good at saving money.

55. I am smart with my money.

56. I am dedicated to saving money.

57. I always find ways to save money.

58. I am in total control of my finances.

59. I closely track my spending habits.

60. I successfully plan my finances and always have left over money to save.

61. I am highly driven and motivated to succeed.

62. I am fully dedicated to growing my wealth.

63. I am on the path to abundance.

64. I have the ability to make large amounts of money.

65. My mind is focused on achieving great wealth.

66. I am starting to effortlessly attract money.

67. I am transforming into someone who effortlessly builds wealth.

68. I am starting to feel more and more confident in my financial abilities.

69. Developing self-belief will help me to achieve my financial goals.

70. I find it easy to pursue my financial goals with confidence.

71. I always find a way to succeed with God.

72. I naturally attract money.

73. Making money is easy for me.

74. I deserve to be rich.

75. Wealth and success are normal for me.

76. Others see me as someone who just naturally attracts money.

77. I enjoy making money.

78. Financial abundance is a normal part of my life.

79. Having a positive attitude towards money is an important part of who I am.

80. I am capable of consistently saving money.

81. I am highly disciplined with my money and never spend it impulsively.

82. I am constantly growing my savings account.

83. I am good at saving money.

84. I am smart with my money.

85. I am dedicated to saving money.

86. I always find ways to save money.

87. I am in total control of my finances.

88. I closely track my spending habits. I am capable of consistently saving money.

89. I am highly disciplined with my money and never spend it impulsively.

90. I am constantly growing my savings account.

91. I find it easy to save money.

92. Saving money is something I enjoy.

93. Proper money management is making it easier to save money.

94. Being smart with my finances comes naturally to me.

95. I am just naturally good at controlling my finances and saving money.

96. Saving money feels good.

97. Being financially responsible is very important to me.

98. People look up to me as someone who is smart with money.

99. Saving money seems effortless.

100. Being in control of my money is making my life better.

101. I am getting out of debt.

102. I always spend money wisely.

103. I know exactly where all of my money is going at all times.

104. I am on top of my finances.

105. I always find a way to put money in to my savings.

106. My mind is highly focused on getting out of debt.

107. I always handle my finances with care and attention.

108. I am in command of my money.

109. I am always disciplined in how I spend my money.

110. I am developing a strong dedication to living a debt free life.

111. I am becoming more responsible with my money.

112. I will get my finances in order.

113. I am starting to effortlessly resist spending money on things I don't need.

114. I am moving towards a debt free life.

115. Each day I am becoming more financially healthy.

116. I will change my spending habits and take control of my money.

117. I will easily get out of debt.

118. I am naturally disciplined with my money.

119. It is important to me that I take control of my finances.

120. I enjoy spending my money wisely.

121. It feels good when I resist the temptation to spend money unnecessarily.

122. I am the kind of person who is just naturally good with my money.

123. Being financially healthy is crucial to my happiness.

124. I can effortlessly visualize what it will feel like to be debt free.

125. Others can see that I am always responsible with my money.

126. I find it easy to save money.

127. I am free from financial self-sabotage.

128. God is my greatest ally.

129. I will be free from negative financial thinking.

130. I am becoming totally focused on achieving my financial goals.

131. I am becoming naturally driven and successful with managing my money.

132. Financial success comes naturally to me.

133. Staying focused on my financial goals is easy.

134. I am finding myself more intensely focused on achieving my financial dreams.

135. I am becoming highly passionate about achieving my financial goals.

136. I find it easy to stay motivated and achieve my financial dreams.

137. I naturally attract financial success.

138. I am a financially productive person.

139. I find it easy to set financial goals and achieve those goals.

140. I am naturally becoming someone who sets high personal financial standards for themselves.

141. I am certain that I will make large amounts of money with God's help and guidance.

142. I will make millions of dollars with God's guidance.

143. I will do whatever God instructs me to do to become a millionaire.

144. I deserve to make millions of dollars.

145. I am motivated to make large amounts of money to help God's people.

146. Becoming a millionaire is something I will just do naturally .

147. I have a natural belief in my ability to create wealth and success.

148. I know I have to work hard to create massive wealth for myself.

149. Becoming a millionaire will happen as long as I keep trying. Focus, discipline, and motivation are easy for me.

150. I am prosperous, wealthy and happy.

151. All the wealth I have brings me joy.

152. I will always have more than enough wealth and prosperity.

153. I am attracting financial prosperity.

154. I am and will always be prosperous.

155. I deserve to prosper.

156. My net worth is always increasing.

157. My wealth is increasing regularly making me prosperous.

158. The whole universe is conspiring to make me prosperous.

159. I am thankful for the prosperity in my life.

160. I am prosperous.

161. Prosperity is my birthright.

162. My life is prosperous.

163. Prosperity is mine.

164. I give generously to myself and others.

165. I see prosperity everywhere.

166. I attract prosperity like a powerful magnet.

167. I give thanks for the prosperity which is mine.

168. Wealth and prosperity are circulating in my life.

169. My circumstances are changing, and prosperity is flowing into my life.

170. I create prosperity in my life.

171. I notice prosperity all around me.

172. Prosperity is mine and I choose to live it.

173. I create prosperity easily and effortlessly.

174. Prosperity is within me, prosperity is around me.

175. I enjoy my prosperity and share it freely with the world.

176. All resistance to prosperity has dissolved in total grace.

177. My prosperity is unlimited, my success is unlimited now.

178. I always have whatever I need. The Universe takes good care of me.

179. Prosperity within me, prosperity around me.

180. I allow all good things to come into my life and I enjoy them.

181. I let go of all resistance to prosperity and it comes to me naturally.

182. Prosperity surrounds me, prosperity fills me and prosperity flows to me and through me.

183. I move from poverty thinking to prosperity thinking and my finances reflect this change.

184. Prosperity of all kinds are drawn to me Now!

185. Every day I grow more financially prosperous!

186. I love prosperity and I attract it naturally.

187. I deserve all good in my life and that includes prosperity.

188. My income is constantly increasing and I prosper wherever I turn!

189. I believe I have the right to be prosperous and successful.

190. I deserve to prosper in everything I do.

191. I can be prosperous.

192. I was prosperous, am prosperous, and will always be prosperous.

193. Every day in every way I am becoming more and more prosperous.

194. Everything and everybody prospers me now.

195. I now draw the highest, best, and most prosperous minded people to me.

196. All resistance to prosperity dissolves away.

197. Prosperity flows to me at all times, in all ways.

198. I allow prosperity.

199. Every day I am growing more financially prosperous.

200. I prosper wherever I turn and I know that I deserve prosperity of all kinds.

201. I accept prosperity and Abundance into my life.

202. I speak of success and prosperity. My words uplift and inspire others.

203. I recognize my true Source and let prosperity pour forth into my every experience.

204. I give thanks that the prosperity which is mine by Divine Right, NOW pours in and piles up under grace in perfect ways.

205. My prosperity is unlimited. My success is unlimited NOW.

206. I am destined to find Prosperity in everything. I do.

207. I know there is ample Prosperity for all.

208. Prosperity now happens to me.

209. I let go of all resistance to Prosperity, and it comes to me naturally.

210. I am worthy of receiving Prosperity now.

211. Prosperity and abundance surround me.

212. I attract Prosperity with each thought I think.

213. I have everything I need right now to accomplish everything I want.

214. The possibilities of the universe are flowing to me.

215. I am safe, all my needs are met.

216. I already have everything I need.

217. I give generously, and receive graciously.

218. My prosperity contributes to the prosperity of others.

219. I am eager to give more than I am paid for.

220. I respect my abilities and always work to my full potential.

221. I am a positive resource and people want to do business with me.

222. All my properties are cash-flow positive.

223. I will be productive and prosperous today.

224. I am prosperous in everything I do.

225. I am prosperous, wealthy and happy.

226. I am easily attracting all the wealth that I desire into my life.

227. Prosperity and abundance comes to me easily and effortlessly.

228. It is easy for me to become prosperous.

229. I am worthy to have abundance and prosperity.

230. I am a magnet to prosperity and abundance.

231. All the wealth I have brings me joy.

232. I will always have more than enough wealth and prosperity.

233. I am attracting financial prosperity.

234. I am, and will always be prosperous.

235. I deserve to prosper.

236. My net worth is always increasing.

237. My wealth is increasing regularly making prosperous.

238. I am thankful for the prosperity in my life.

239. I am prosperous.

240. Prosperity is my birthright.

241. My life is prosperous.

242. Prosperity is mine.

243. I give generously to myself and others.

244. I see prosperity everywhere.

245. I attract prosperity like a powerful magnet.

246. I give thanks for the prosperity which is mine.

247. Wealth and prosperity are circulating in my life.

248. My circumstances are changing and prosperity is flowing into my life.

249. I create prosperity in my life.

250. I notice prosperity all around me.

251. Prosperity is mine and I choose to live it.

252. I create prosperity easily and effortlessly.

253. Prosperity is within me, prosperity is around me.

254. I enjoy my prosperity and share it freely with the world.

255. All resistance to prosperity has dissolved in total grace.

256. My prosperity is unlimited, my success is unlimited now.

257. I was prosperous, am prosperous and will always be prosperous.

258. I always have whatever I need. God takes good care of me.

259. My life is full of love, joy, and all the material things that I need.

260. Prosperity is within me, prosperity is around me.

261. I allow all good things to come into my life and I enjoy them.

262. I let go of all resistance to prosperity and it comes to me naturally.

263. Prosperity surrounds me, prosperity fills me and prosperity flows to me and through me.

264. I move from poverty thinking to prosperity thinking and my finances reflect this change.

265. I now release the gold-mine within me. I am linked with an endless golden stream of prosperity which comes to me under grace in perfect ways.

266. Prosperity of all kinds are drawn to me Now!

267. Every day I grow more financially prosperous!

268. I love prosperity and I attract it naturally.

269. I deserve all good in my life and that includes prosperity

270. My income is constantly increasing and I prosper wherever I turn!

271. I believe I have the right to be prosperous and successful.

272. I deserve to prosper in everything I do.

273. It is so easy to open to prosperity.

274. I can be prosperous.

275. I was prosperous, am prosperous and will always be prosperous.

276. All resistance to prosperity dissolves away.

277. Prosperity flows to me at all times, in all ways.

278. Everyday I am growing more financially prosperous.

279. I prosper wherever I turn and I know that I deserve prosperity of all kinds.

280. I am happy, healthy, and prosperous.

281. My prosperity prospers others.

282. I trust the universal spirit of prosperity to provide richly for me now.

283. I accept prosperity and Abundance into my life.

284. I speak of success and prosperity. My words uplift and inspire others.

285. I recognize my true Source and let prosperity pour forth into my every experience.

286. My prosperity is unlimited. My success is unlimited NOW.

287. I am destined to find Prosperity in everything I do.

288. I know there is ample Prosperity for all.

289. I let go of all resistance to Prosperity, and it comes to me naturally.

290. I am worthy of receiving Prosperity now.

291. Prosperity and abundance surround me.

292. I attract Prosperity with each thought I think.

293. I have everything I need right now to accomplish everything I want.

294. I am safe, all my needs are met.

295. I have everything I need to get everything I want.

296. I deserve the good life.

297. I give generously, and receive graciously.

298. My prosperity contributes to the prosperity of others.

299. I am eager to give more than I am paid for.

300. I am a positive resource and people want to do business with me.

301. All my properties are cash-flow positive.

302. I am living an abundantly happy life.

303. I can see abundance everywhere around me.

304. I absolutely attract abundance.

305. I believe that more abundance is coming to me now.

306. I am easily led to the abundance I desire.

307. I am deserving of abundance, no matter what.

308. I allow the Universe to bless me with great abundance now.

309. My good now flows to me in streams of success, happiness, and abundance.

310. I deserve to have financial abundance in my life now.

311. I enjoy an abundance of money.

312. Abundance flows easily when I relax.

313. Abundance is my divine birthright. Today I expand my awareness of the abundance around me.

314. Perfect abundance is my chosen reality.

315. Abundance flows to me.

316. I am thankful for the abundance in my life.

317. I love abundance and I attract it naturally.

318. I believe I have the right to be abundant, and successful.

319. I will live life abundantly.

320. I will live the abundant life.

321. All my needs are met instantaneously.

322. My mind is a powerful magnet for riches and abundance.

323. I AM Unlimited! I AM Abundant! I AM Worthy and Deserving of All Good!

324. Cash moves in abundant amounts in my Life!

325. I always have more than enough of everything I need.

326. My income is constantly increasing.

327. My good comes from everywhere and everyone.

328. New opportunities to increase my income open up for me now.

329. I am overflowing with Abundant Prosperity!

330. Abundance is my birthright and I have it.

331. Abundance within me, abundance around me.

332. I now realize my plan for abundant living.

333. The more grateful I am, the more reasons I find to be grateful.

334. I pay my bills with love as I know abundance flows freely through me.

335. Abundance surrounds me. Today I claim my share.

336. I have Abundance to share and to spare.

337. I expect lavish Abundance every day in every way in my life and affairs.

338. I welcome and enthusiastically accept unlimited Abundance.

339. My financial Abundance overflows today.

340. My life is filled with an Abundance of good.

341. With God to guide me, my life is filled with joyous successes and rich Abundance.

342. I release all feelings of lack and limitation, and joyfully accept blessings of joy and Abundance.

343. Abundance is mine! I give thanks for the unlimited flow of good into my life.

344. Gratitude moves me from perceptions of lack to manifestations of Abundance in all facets of my life.

345. God is the source of my Abundance.

346. I deserve Abundance.

347. I have Abundance in every area of my life.

348. I bless the Abundance I see in others.

349. I live in an abundant universe. I always have everything I need.

350. I am abundantly provided for as I follow God.

351. I choose to live an abundant life.

352. My greatest good is coming to me now.

353. Today is filled with opportunity, and I will seize it.

354. Everything good is coming to me easily and effortlessly.

355. I can, and will have more than I ever dreamed possible.

356. Like a powerful magnet, I attract all my desires in great abundance.

357. I am certain that my path is always perfect for me.

358. God has given me everything I need to achieve every goal I have.

359. I am a grateful person receiving the abundant blessings of God.

360. I have unlimited potential. Only good lies before me.

361. I am open and receptive to all the good and abundance in the universe. Thank you Creator.

362. My life flows effortlessly as doors of opportunity open to me everywhere in every aspect of my life.

363. Abundance flows through me.

364. My bank account is filled by God. As soon as I release money, money is released back to me 100-fold.

365. I release all resistance to attracting money. I am worthy of a positive cashflow.

About The Author

Rhea is founder of, Not Your Average Church Lady which seeks to encourage inspire and promote women to be their absolute best selves and who God has destined them to be. She holds Masters degrees in Sports Administration and Marriage & Family Therapy, as well as, a Bachelor of Arts in Criminal Justice & Sociology from Canisius College. Rhea currently works as Marriage & Family Therapist. She has been married to her husband, Ricky for 12 years. Together they have 5 growing sons.

www.ingramcontent.com/pod-product-compliance
Lightning Source LLC
Chambersburg PA
CBHW052103110526
44591CB00013B/2335